Talk To Me

The Unstoppable Power of R.E.A.L. Conversational Sales

By: Gary Gale Norris

PUBLISHED IN THE UNITED STATES OF AMERICA.

Dedication

To God: When it comes to conversation, listening, grace, mercy, relationship, empathy, action and life, no one can compare to how you have walked with me through all of the above. It has been your kind hands that have drawn in the sand for me many times ... and I am so very grateful. Thank you for being so patient with me. I have done my best to wreck our relationship but you never gave up on me. I have learned through our conversations ... that your love for me is far greater than my mistakes. I love you for loving me first and best.

To Bud McFadden: My first employer. When you saw my dad bring that wide-eyed kid through your Western Auto door, I know you thought I was just like every other kid who needed a summer job to put gas in his car; but even still, you went a bit further. You believed in me. You gave me courage to believe in myself. As you saw me working, you gave me more and more responsibility which groomed the work ethic my father and grandfather had instilled in me early. No matter where I go or what I accomplish, it all started with that hot summer day when you shook my dad's hand and said, "Sure, we can put him to work." You could have said no. I am so glad that you didn't. Thank you, Bud McFadden, for taking a chance on me. I am forever grateful.

To My Grandfather, Edsel Greene: As far back as I can remember, the one thing I can say I always saw you doing, was working. Always on the go, always a furnace to fix in the dead of winter or a garden to hoe or a fruit tree to cover because frost was coming. As I have gotten older, I have also grown to see a different side of you. It's a part of your nature that I have grown to appreciate. Your love for history is inspiring and I think you passed this on to me. Thank you, Grandpa. The past is where we can look back to discover the original architect's intention. I remember your stories of mountain folk paying the doctor, the preacher (and anyone else to whom a debt was owed), and they would make their payments in milk, eggs and fried chicken. I also remember the stores of negotiation and bartering. From those stories and a thousand like them, this book was born. Thank you for taking the time to tell me those stories and I look forward to many more. I love you, Grandpa.

Table of Contents

Author's Note

Humans detest being manipulated, coerced, and otherwise hoodwinked into anything. I have been in sales, myself, and I can't think of a single time it was enjoyable - at least not the way I was instructed to execute it or the way success was defined. I was on the inside, shoulder-to-shoulder with the ones who were getting all the plaques and awards. What I noticed about these individuals, was that they were all tormented too. They carried loads of guilt and wore many scars. They were often dealing with a broken relationship - or about to. The carnage behind them was due to too many work hours and less than favorable habits. But, they were wearing the Italian leather shoes and the Brooks Brothers suits. They were featured on the walls as the superstar. I can count on one hand the number of sales professionals I have known personally who didn't carry a ton of baggage from their career. Yet, deep inside, they wanted to do better. They were seeking a better way. I have heard them say, "Unless you are cut-throat around here, you will starve." Why does it have to be that way?

This is why I wrote this book.

I have closed very large sales and very small sales without

reverting to the tactics that caused so much angst and suffering in so many of my colleagues' lives. It is my hope that the reader will see the origin of sales as an integrity-riveted profession, and that it longs to be so, still. If you happen to enjoy sales with coercion, pressured closes, shallow scripts and overt body language ... I wish you all the best. If you just love the idea and energy of the sales profession and are looking for a way to ascend while keeping your consciences intact, I hope you will find what you are looking for in the pages ahead. The principles contained here have set me free to be successful in sales, while also being genuinely myself. Wherever you land at the end of this book, I am pulling for you and praying you are blessed with all the best your career has to offer.

Gary

Preface

Why? It's a question that, in some instances, must be asked and answered when determining our motivation for starting a business. When considering the course of action we are about to take; when counting the cost of launching out into the deep; we must ask ourselves why - and we must return an answer that satisfies the insatiable instinct in us to either step out, or remain in the safety of the boat. In this book, I hope to provide an answer to the following questions: Why is sales such an integrity-challenged industry? Why are sales people so stereotypically untrusted and misunderstood? Did it start out that way? What was the original architect's intention? I think at the very least, I will be able to provoke introspective thought concerning this most misunderstood, yet imperative, profession. Over the course of my career, people have commented that my technique for negotiating and closing sales seems natural - but I would rather call it conversational. I endeavor to unpack this idea of conversational sales, one section at a time. Hopefully, you will see at the end of this journey, that the greatest gift you have in successful sales ... is you.

CHAPTER 1

Welcome to the Jungle

Yes. Welcome to the jungle is a fitting description of the entire sales experience, for both buyer and seller. In many ways, it truly resembles a "survival of the fittest" sort of scenario. Here's the image:

The buyer sees something he wants or needs. He slowly and stealthily meanders to the price tag, acting as if interest is minimal and need is irrelevant. Possibly, a smug sigh follows as something is muttered under his breath. Body language would indicate that genuine interest and need are both at an all time low. Any lower and the buyer would fall into a lethargic state that not even life support paddles could reverse. Then, there is the Salesperson. A master of manipulation. A sage of reading minds and body language. His target is in sight. He moves slowly in and suddenly with a swift first strike, his outstretched business card slices the air like a knife and he cordially offers to answer any questions you may have. The trap has been set. The prey is hovering around the trap, as if to taunt the predator. Slowly but surely, the helpless antelope is unable to resist the temptation to haggle and says, "I do have one question." SNAP! The Salesperson leaps for the jugular and responds, "Sure!" It's there that struggle begins. Some days, the struggle ends with the buyer escaping due to his resilience in demanding a discount and the salesperson not being able to accomodate or unwilling to compromise price for fear of what other stronger sales people might say. The buyer feels as though they have survived to haggle again. Yet on other days, the Salesperson wins the struggle due solely to their ability to manipulate emotions, urgency, scarcity and value. The poor buyer leaves with something they do not need, can't remember how they got it, are stuck with explaining why they spent so much and feel oppressive levels of remorse that they have made a mistake. *What a mess!* Now, before I go any further. This is not always the case. I am not this kind of buyer or salesperson. I know what I need. I don't need to be swayed. I also find out very quickly what my client needs. That is all I will offer them. Not a sliver more. But for the rest of the world, the jungle analogy depicts exactly what the sales cycle looks like.

Why must the sales process be like this? Was it always this way? What should it look like? I will endeavor over the next few lines to explain what has happened (in my opinion of course), and how the world of sales began, from my perspective, of course. Then, we will take a look at my intention for this book.

The Basics of How Sales Began
The Beginning … Literally.

Bartering is truly the oldest known form of exchange. Livestock, land, textiles, herbs, crops, tools, ships, water, salt, spices, information, labor, protections and even armies were forms of "goods" or "services". At this early age of development, the exchange was driven by need alone, and what goods or services best met the genuine need. If I didn't need 25 head of cattle, there was no desire or attempt by the keeper of herds to exchange the cattle for my land, or water rights, or whatever I have to barter. It may be offered, but if cattle held no value for me, declining the offer was accepted and respected. Remember this statement: the exchange of goods or services for goods or services was predicated and accomplished successfully, based *only* on **genuine need.**

The Introduction of Currency: BC - AD

Enter all known uses of currency, from the Aztecs to the Roman Empire. Currency was a valuable means of tracking the receipt of goods and services, and the satisfactory relevant authority (city, state, national) assured means of "value exchange" or what we know today as payment. To use our earlier example, if I were interested in 25 head of cattle, but didn't have any land, water, sheep, salt or anything of value that I wanted to part with as payment, or the seller didn't need, I could provide a relevant authority assured currency to the keeper of cattle as a means of payment, with the guarantee the the keeper of cattle could use the currency anywhere in the marketplace and it would be honored and exchanged for equally valued goods or services.

Role Specialization - Insurances: 1750s to 1850s

Historians agree, we can thank Benjamin Franklin for both insurance and the insurance sales profession. During this era, a trained salesperson, representing the insurance company, would make house calls to assess the insurance needs of families, present a pitch of appropriate coverages and protections, and would "close the sale" (in that day, this meant finalizing and acceptance of the offering) commensurate with levels of insurance, for a monthly subscription or recurring fee. Then, they would return monthly to collect the subscription fee and have a cup of tea or coffee. This was a process called role specialization.

Thanks to Ben, we identified electricity and a new profession that has stood the test of time. This is also the era where competition was introduced. Whoever could make the best case for their insurance, would get the subscription fee. Interesting.

Snake Oil … Yep, it was a Thing: 1850s to 1920s

Ok. Seriously? Yes, seriously. It was a real liquid that could be purchased and it had real rattlesnake venom in it. Railroad workers would purchase this to rub on their sore muscles. The venom would temporarily numb the pain, giving it a "miracle cure" reputation. The man we have to thank for this is Clark Stanley, heralded as the original snake oil salesman. As competition became heated, the claims of healing properties became outrageous. This continued until 1917 when he was ordered to stop selling his oil and was fined. The strange thing is this; sales as a profession has evolved, but the reputation of gum popping, finger pistol pointing, smooth talking salespeople and the over the top manipulative tactics and miraculous claims, haven't. Remember the introduction of competition? Here it rears its ugly head again. But this time, with a vengeance.

IBM & The Psychology of Selling - E.K. Strong: Mid

1920s to the Mid 1930s

In 1924, Thomas J. Watson Sr. began International Business Machines (IBM) based on the ideology that a professional "sales force" could be deployed to honestly and effectively represent the interests of both company and consumer. His principles maintained that this force must be educated, professional and well-trained. Then, in 1925, E.K. Strong published, *The Psychology of Selling*. Now this is sounding more familiar. In his book, Strong proposed several closing techniques, open-ended questions, features and benefit comparisons, and other engagement methods still in practice today. The book was a foundation shaker when it was published and it changed the game. Sales became more than snake oil and insurance policies. It became a profession that anyone could master through education and training. Within the next 10 years, Dale Carnegie would publish his book, *How to Make Friends and Influence People*. Laying out the now famous AIDCA formula (Attention, Interest, Desire, Conviction, Action), Carnegie shows sales professionals how to take buyers through the stages of making a buying commitment.

SPIN & Solution Selling: 1980s

Yep - sounding real familiar now. This era took

open-ended questions and transformed them into the ultimate mind game. The premise of SPIN selling is that your buyer has a need for your product or service, even if they don't realize it. The more sequenced questions you ask, the more likely you are to reveal an undiscovered need and close the sale. This method makes me want to wash my hands in gasoline and light them on fire, even as I write it. Then, solution selling happens when the salesperson listens long enough to hear a need, and then moves to meet that need. This is more akin to the beginning but still a long shot away. I cut my teeth in sales as this era was coming to a close. My first sales job was as a copier salesperson. I had to listen to the cassettes of Brian Tracy and Zig Zieglar for hours. I read their books and passed their courses. I remember this season of my life very well, but not with very fond memories.

CRMs and SaaS: 2011 to Now

The internet and application-development has propelled sales into a new galaxy. Thanks to Aaron Ross and the innovators of our present day, more time is spent closing deals and less time cultivating prospects. I use CRM systems myself. My staff uses them. They are invaluable. I am grateful for Mr. Ross's contributions. They help those of us who are trying to honor the origins of sales the way it was created to be.

Let's recap what I believe has brought us to the present day.

When we take an inventory of landmarks that have impacted the landscape of sales, we see three corrosive "C's":

1. Currency: The ability to acquire or release goods and services without the barter of the valuable goods and services. The removal of expressed need. Now, the acquisition is made on desire or the power to purchase. No currency, no purchase. Currency will always be part of sales; however, expressed genuine need in later years, has all but disappeared.

2. Competition: The salesperson with the most compelling pitch, outrageous claim, entertaining presentation, or emotionally manipulative plea, wins the sale. Say whatever needs to be said in order to inflate the value of my product or service *and* discredit my competitor. No holds barred. Close the deal at all costs - even if this cost falls to the buyer.

3. Coercion: A sales process that gets into your head. They will talk you into believing that you have a need you didn't even realize you had. Through the masterful application of open ended questions, pressurized scenarios, and apocalyptic ultimatums, our feeble minds will bend to their will. Then, when you wake tomorrow, a little poorer, realizing what has happened, remorse will set in. Upon questioning your actions, you will discover that your purchase is "no return - no refund". Now this is quite overstated but on the buying end, it feels just like this.

In my opinion, when genuine need is present, closing techniques are useless. If you are in sales, you would call this type of sale a "lay down". No fight. This is the most disrespected type of sale among snake oil salespeople. When genuine need is present, open-ended questions are awkward and unnecessary. Features and benefits are requested by the buyer, not used as leverage for pressure by the salesperson. What history shows us is this; the introduction of currency, competition and coercion over the history of sales has changed what the architect envisioned for a salesperson. In my humble opinion, these three elements have polluted and poisoned this honorable profession. My hope is that this book will begin laying bricks that will restore the original model of sales and return honor and honesty to this oldest of professions. It is my hope and prayer that through the power of simple, honest and humble conversation, you will see that there is no place in true sales for psychological, emotional or unrealized-need manipulation. I hope you see that in the beginning, a neighbor came because they needed help. We had the power to help, and we did. Need and Supply. Both can be satisfied through conversation. Ladies and Gentlemen, fellow salespeople, dear readers, I hope in the coming pages, to make a compelling case for the unstoppable power of ***conversational sales.***

NOTES & TAKEAWAYS

1. Where did sales begin?

2. What are the "C"s that impacted changed sales forever?

3. Who is the father of sales, as a profession?

CHAPTER 2

What is Conversation?

Let's go back to the beginning. You will hear that phrase a lot in this book. If you start with the definition of a conversation, you will see variations of this central theme; a conversation is a talk, especially an informal one, between two or more people, in which news and ideas are exchanged. Interesting. Seems harmless enough. The cover of this book is my grandpa and me having a conversation. If I remember correctly, we were discussing successful strategies for sawmilling from the depression era. He is a history buff. We had an informal, safe, transparent conversation. Yet sales engagements today are classified as anything but informal, low key, safe, comfortable, equal, exchanges of news or ideas. Did the last visit you made to the local car dealership feel like this? Did the last visit to a furniture store feel like this? Did the last computer purchase or appliance purchase feel like this? Probably not. Especially if you found yourself at a big box store, teeming with a "salesforce" whose bonus depended on whether or not they could overpower you mentally with pressure or open-ended questions. I can tell you what it most likely wasn't. It wasn't a conversation.

When we get together with those we trust most, these

anomalies can be found in almost every room of the gathering place. Conversations. A safe and equal exchange of news or ideas. You weren't being sized up for some great closing question or mentally / emotionally manipulated. A healthy exchange of how someone is doing, how their family is doing, or an exchange about local happenings that are noteworthy. We all have an aunt or uncle who has opinions about this or that and aren't afraid to share them. Still safe, yet heard and received with a gentle smile and a shake of the head. Can you think of the last time you had a conversation in a sales environment? Just a chat really. It's such a rare thing to find. Why is this? Why does going to the used car lot to find a vehicle for my son have to begin with a self-focused pep rally to not buy a lemon. To not be bullied. To not leave with something I don't want. To not be taken advantage of when the lot attendant tells me my trade in isn't worth anything. To have my guard up because Fast-Eddie will get one over on you if you're not careful. Why can't my son and I just stop in, have a coffee with the lot attendant, talk sports and business, and discuss the genuine expressed needs my son has in a vehicle? Will this ever be the case? Could it be the case?

It can be. It is in my world. You should check it out. I like it over here. I think you will, too. I have an exercise for you. This will work even for us introverts. Yes. I am an introvert *and* I am a sales professional. How is that possible? You will learn in this book. Hang in there we will get to that. Now, that exercise I mentioned. This exercise does have one requirement: genuine need. Identify something you genuinely need. It could be a car, a house, a storage building, a tractor, a business suit, a laptop, etc. Identify something you genuinely need. Then, select the purveyor of those needs based on competence to meet that need. It may be a small local business. Once you have identified the need and the local merchant with the capacity to meet the need, go there. But, go differently this time. Go with the mindset to have a conversation. To experience the safe and equal exchange of news (needs - its news to them) and ideas (how and when you intend to purchase). When you do, I would love to hear your stories. Please, take a minute and email them to me at garygale@norrisventures.com. I will be highlighting them in our blogs from time to time. See, this is where true sales success happens. When an environment is created where the safe, equal, and honest exchange of ideas and news is the basis for sales engagement, there will not be enough time in the day to serve the customers that will flood the floor space. If you own a business that employs sales people, I encourage you, start now creating this environment. Start now cultivating a salesforce that engages on this level. The level of conversation.

NOTES & TAKEAWAYS

1. What is the basic definition of conversation?

2. Can you remember a sales engagement that genuinely progressed along the lines of a conversation?

3. Name someone who you really enjoy having a conversation with. Think about how the elements of those conversations convert to a sales engagement.

CHAPTER 3

Closing = Trapping

Close. Closing. Closes. It's really kind of a negative word. The application of this word to the sales process is less than positive at the very least. How many times have you heard, "I closed them." referring to an individual who was bested in a match of wits and resistance? How about, "I closed the deal." referring to a battle of wills with only one winner. Or this one, "(He/She) just got closed!" On various occasions in sales jobs of my past, I recall checking in with my managers to relay progress and getting the response: "Gary, close the freakin' deal!" or "Now, go close the deal!" Why did the deal need closing? Did my manager care if the buyer needed what I was selling, or not? Did the buyer actually need what I was selling, or not? Warning: *slight sarcasm ahead.* Maybe the buyer was just previously unaware of this great need I had been able to uncover in a single hour, not even having ever met this person before; not hurting with them in their pain; not celebrating with them in their victories; not feeding them when they were hungry or providing water when they were thirsty. But somehow, *somehow*, I had been able to identify a need that this person in front of me had, that they had no idea they had. So, based on my ace "sales training", my manager expected my next steps to be a picture painted heavily of impending doom if the buyer didn't bite and a stressed expression of this need until it crushed the buyer into powder, rendering them paralysed to resist my verbal and mental prowess. They would have no choice but to succumb to my intellect and uncanny understanding of their needs. Then, in the final moments of struggle - the closing blow (probably a "take away close" yep, I went there) and the deal would be sealed. Closing accomplished. The trap was set, and the prey was captured. And scene: *sarcasm concluded.*

So, close the deal? Why are closes necessary? The sales process and cycle proposed in this book shows that closes are not necessary. There is absolutely no need for me to enter into an aggressive posture of closing if genuine need truly exists. Does genuine need truly exist? Why not spend more time qualifying genuine needs than posturing and positioning? I want to spend the next few lines clarifying what genuine need looks like. This will lay the foundation for my conviction that closes were created to gain a strategic advantage in sales during the 1930's amid The Great Depression to offset the competition created in this new and exploding profession. But now, they are not.

What is genuine need? I want to place the above scenario into a more personal context for you, the reader. I am going to choose my own mother. Why? Because she and my father rank among the most important and dear people to me on earth. I am choosing my mother instead of my father because she is a traditional woman; a homemaker. To some, she might seem an easy target to be closed. I want you, the reader, to put the most precious person in your life right now, into this scenario and let's see where we land.

My mother has suffered with sarcoidosis for a very long time now. This disease weakens her lungs, reduces her breathing capacity and impedes her quality of life, every day. But, my mom is a fighter. She doesn't give up easily. Every day she has to keep a steroid inhaler close by because the attacks are unpredictable. Her genuine need are these steroid inhalers. Now, imagine that she comes to me needing a replacement because she is having an attack and has just realized that her inhaler is empty. Do I need to close her on what she genuinely needs? *No!* First of all, I would never think of entering into a negotiation about inhalers at this moment. Why? Her need is genuine and obvious. Second, she would never question my suggestion as to where and how to acquire that inhaler. She would be fully compliant and the pricing would be minimally, if at all, discussed. Can you imagine my mother coming to me at this moment? Her struggle to take her next breath is evident. She barely has enough breath to express her need. Now, imagine that I take her through all of the options of inhalers, price points, features and benefits, and end with, "How will you be paying today, cash or credit card?" Ludicrous right? I hope you are getting the imagery. This is extreme. But imagine your loved one coming to you with a genuine need. Would you walk them through a closing process or would you move heaven and earth to meet their needs? You would most likely do whatever is necessary and would run over anyone who attempted to prevent you from meeting that expressed and evident need. Money and pricing would be no object. It wouldn't even be a part of the conversation for either of you. They have a need that only you can meet. You are going to meet that need no matter what. Do you see the ridiculous proposition of closing when true genuine expressed need is present?

Now, let's bring down the volume for a minute. Take the facets of genuine need and lay them as a filter over your last sales experience. A prospect engaged with you concerning an expressed or implied need. Instead of focusing on budget or a quick sales cycle, what if you were to focus on the genuine need? A true empathic understanding of the buyer in front of you and what their genuine needs really are. If there isn't a genuine need, *do not* fabricate urgency. Your responsibility is to provide all the information they will need to make the best decision they can possibly make. In the scenario of my mother, if her breathing were fine and she were just "shopping" for inhalers, I would never think to fabricate urgency to manipulate her into buying something she doesn't need. I would simply provide her with all the options and would most likely look for the best value for her money. Most modern day sales managers will not allow that. But, it is the only morally-sound response to someone who does not *yet* have a genuine need. They are simply and truly shopping. Be the best at preparing them for the moment when the urgency is real. If you do that, your name and help will be the first thing they think of when the urgency is real and a buying decision must be made. What I am trying to say is this: when genuine need is present, closes are horrible, manipulative mind games that are grossly unnecessary. When genuine need is not present, your mission is to provide the seeker with as much relevant data to help them make the best and wisest decision when genuine need *is* present. I can hear some of you now, *"But what if I lose the sale?"* You won't, at least not in the long-term. It's a lie of this sales industry that the most aggressive salesperson wins. They don't. The most genuine guide gains a place in the story. Guides are the buyer's safety net for the journey. They have walked the path before. They know where the cliffs are. They know where to set up camp. They know which indigenous plants that can be eaten. They know where to fish. They have all the pertinent information. If you are the guide, it would be foolish for your prospect to select a salesperson who hasn't, first, been their guide. Guiding buyers is where trust is born. My mother trusts me because she knows I will put her needs and goals first. Not my own. Did your last sales engagement end that way? Did your prospect leave *knowing* that their needs and goals were priority one with you? I hope so.

To conclude, never forget: when genuine need is present, closes are not needed. When genuine need is not present, guide your buyer to all the most relevant information and

then when the genuine need arrives, they will trust you for
the journey.

NOTES & TAKEAWAYS

1. Why is closing described as trapping in this chapter?

2. List closing techniques you are familiar with.

3. When genuine need is present, _____.

CHAPTER 4

Scripts = Premeditation

Now, let's talk about scripts. You know, those uncomfortable role playing exercises we all had to force ourselves to partake in? The all-too familiar, *"Let's just say…"* kind of situations that only teach a deeper level of premeditated manipulation? Yeh, those. It is a sales-muscle remembrance exercise that quickly leads to moral carpal tunnel. Here is why I say that. Imagine that you are about to have a chat with a dear friend. They have asked for some time to talk to you about a genuine need they have and they are confident that you will be able to help them navigate their need. They will be meeting with you tomorrow at noon for lunch. So for the next several hours, you begin to rehearse scripts of conversations that might accomplish *your* purpose. You even write scripts that might "canal" the conversation in a direction of your choosing. Sounds disgusting, right? Why would you ever do this? You wouldn't. You would meet them promptly at noon. You would exchange as genuine friends do: "How are you?" and "How are the kids?" and "What did you think of the game?" and things like that. There would be no rehearsal or scripting of the conversation. It would be a natural, safe, equal exchange of news or ideas (conversation).

You may be saying, "Yeh, but this is my dear friend. I don't know my prospects." Uh ... you should! You can! You must! I'm not saying that it will be to the level or intimacy of a close friend, but you must still establish a *knowing-of* your prospects for the exchange to be genuine. How robotic and weird it would be to attempt to have a conversation with a friend that was fueled by a canned script. Again, let me stress to you, the reader, where genuine need cohabitates with genuine interest in meeting that need, premeditated scripts are useless. This method of scripted prospect engagement has been drastically abused in the telemarketing industry. It has made its way into email marketing. It has even (believe it or not) made its way into in-person engagement. Doesn't it sound ridiculous to attempt to "script" how you will respond to prospects? You can't. There is only genuine need and a genuine interest in meeting that need. That's it. Nothing more - nothing less. I have taught our staff to engage on the level of genuine need. If you know your solutions, then predicting need will be a waste of time. If you invest yourself in the understanding of your solutions and how they meet genuine needs, you will need no script. The result will be ... wait for it ... a safe and equal exchange of news or ideas. Yep. A conversation. Can you script a safe and equal exchange of ideas? No; at least not with any discernible success or without making the conversation extremely uncomfortable and awkward. And, I doubt seriously that either party will look forward to the next feeble attempt to predict what the other will say or do.

Ugh. Can we not just talk about it? If I tried to script my next conversation with a friend, it would fail. Why try to teach salespeople scripts? The reason is simply this: to teach salespeople the dark art of verbal manipulation in order to accomplish a one-sided advantage. Why not teach them to have conversations? Why not teach them the power of genuine need and the power of a genuine desire to meet that need? Can you talk to your friends? If your friends called you and asked you to help them with a genuine need, would you struggle to do all in your power to meet that need? Genuinely? *And*, the very reason your friends and family reach out to you is because they know you will put their needs at the top of your to do list - that you will carefully listen to their expressed need and then will take whatever action necessary to meet the genuine need.

I know this may sound harsh. I know you may be saying to

yourself, "I didn't have a choice in my scripting training." I know that might be true; however, you have a choice now. And if you will heed the principles I am revealing, I am confident that you will have more new sales and repeat sales than those employing these other tactics. Tactics are for war. Who wins a war? No one. And there are always casualties. Collateral damage. Do you want war with your prospects? I would say you don't. Then why use tactics to achieve a one-sided end? Can't we focus only on practices and outcomes that are win/win ? No war. Only the peaceful meeting of genuine needs with genuine solutions.

In conclusion, where genuine need cohabitates with a genuine desire to meet that expressed need, scripts are unnecessary. All your prospects are looking for is a conversation; a safe equal exchange of news or ideas, where both purveyor and prospect accomplish equal ends.

NOTES & TAKEAWAYS

1. Scripts are _____.

2. Write your thoughts about the role of scripts in your professional and personal relationships. Do you struggle in genuine conversations?

3. Who are the winners in a war? Think about your own sales practices. Do you feel that you and your customers end in a win/win scenario? Why or why not?

CHAPTER 5

Let's Keep it R.E.A.L.

I have gone to great lengths, thus far, to eradicate the school of thought which has predicated and equipped the majority of this generation of sales people with one tool: manipulation of mind, word and emotion. I have established the foundational truth that where genuine need coexists with genuine desire to meet the need, accurately and specifically, that manipulation of any kind is futile and unnecessary. So if the previous methods of sales aren't the right way, what is? I am glad you asked.

Over the last 30 years of closing many large and small deals as well as losing large and small deals, I have created a simple acronym for remembering when you are in a sales engagement situation. If you remember this helpful strategy, you will win in the sales community. Not every time, but enough to know that this approach is time tested from the very beginning of exchanging goods and services for goods and services to this moment in time, right now. I have learned that there are 4 qualities to every successful relationship. Every win/win relationship has these 4 elements present. Without even one of them, you will not win and neither will the other party. All 4 must be present. In your sales career, I always will always encourage you to *keep it* **R.E.A.L.** What does **R.E.A.L.** stand for? Let's unpack this a little more and then I will attempt to unpack them comprehensively in the coming chapters.

R = Relationship

No successful exchange of goods and services for currency will ever occur without a cornerstone of relationship. What do I mean? Unless there is the common ground of, "I acknowledge that I (the salesperson) am willing to invest my time and attention to listen to your needs. I will sit down with you as long as it takes to discover your needs. If we discover together that this is not a need yet, I am committing to you, in this relationship, that I will equip you with as much valuable and relevant information and knowledge as is needed to make the best decision for yourself when this does become a need". Relationship. It is what drives me to make sure my mother has the exact right medicine at the right time. It is what drives us to help our grandparents when they are unable to help themselves. It is what drives us to carry the groceries for the widow down the street. It is what drives us to seek a higher power. It is what drives us to seek a partner in life. *Relationship.* Without establishing this first cornerstone in your sales career, you will not succeed in a way that is in keeping with integrity and will be forced to make greater claims about your snake oil than the next snake oil salesperson to win.

E = Empathy

Ok. It is one thing to build a relationship with your prospective customers/clients and to be still enough to hear the genuine need. It is entirely another thing to identify with the need. Empathy is different from sympathy. Occasionally I will meet a salesperson who has a measure of sympathy. But, sympathy will only take you so far. You can feel sympathy and not ever identify with the need. You must be able to identify with the fruit of the need. Here is what I mean. If need is the "root" then the impact of need, is the "fruit". I will unpack this in detail in the chapter dedicated to empathy. Please remember, unless you identify on a real and relevant level with the need and its impact on the customer/client, you will not be able to successfully provide a solution to the need.

A = Action

Yes! You have built a relationship strong enough to hear the genuine need. You have a genuine desire to meet the need with accuracy. You have identified with the need and its impact on your customer/client. If those cornerstones are in place, the natural next step is *action*. Do something about it! Don't talk about it. Don't overshoot it. Don't bandage it together. Meet the need with accuracy. You have heard. You have identified. Now, provide the solution that fits. In the example of my mother earlier, my relationship and empathy with her cause me to do everything in my power to meet her needs with accuracy. Unless all of the sales training and seminars have seared your conscience and have made you a hollow shell, you will jump at the chance to meet that need. If it is not a need yet, you will jump at the chance to provide all relevant and helpful information to meet that need when the desire becomes a need. It is the natural progression of a real relationship.

L = LIFE

Many of you will be saying, "What does Gary mean here?" Life means a few things which I will also unpack in the chapter dedicated to this last and important final cornerstone. Life means that first of all, you are willing to walk with them after the sale is completed. Life means that you will remain in contact with them after the sale is completed to ensure that the solution you provided was in fact accurate and exact. Life means that your intentions are to help them assimilate into the solution in a way that creates longevity of use and eradicates buyers remorse. By the way, buyer's remorse disappears when you utilize my approach to sales. Life means you are there for the customer/client, no matter what. When I commit to do life with my family, it is *no matter what*. Are you that committed to your customers/clients? Do they know it? Are they aware of your commitment to make sure their needs are met for the long haul? If you are not, they will know it and you will not keep them as a customer/client. They will find someone who does care enough to stick around. To lock arms with them for their needs. To be their go-to for all things _____ (fill in the blank).

Are you prepared to keep it **R.E.A.L.**? I hope so. If you are, keep on reading. The next few pages could transform your career and your life.

NOTES & TAKEAWAYS

1. What does the acronym **R.E.A.L.** stand for?

2. Name the person in your life who really represents a true genuine relationship to you. Think about the things that make it so. How can you translate that to your sales life?

3. Which letter of this acronym raises the most questions inside you? Write it down now so you can compare it to what you learn by the end of this book.

CHAPTER 6

R = Relationship

It's the first step in everything. The first building block for anything with depth and meaning is relationship. It's what would cause me to get up at 3am and drive an hour and a half to pick up medicine for a sick family member. Relationship. It's what would push me to sacrifice a Saturday to help a cousin remodel a kitchen. It's what would press me to dry out a neighbor's flooded basement. Relationship. Whether my relationship is directly with the person in need or only with the God who supplies my needs, relationship is where it all begins. Without it, we have no basis for empathy and action.

I bring this to light because too often in sales engagements, the buyer is asked to make a decision where the relationship is absent. It doesn't work. Let me drive it home a little further. Let's say you are walking through the grocery store filling your cart, as you go, with the things that you and your family need. You know their needs. You are meeting their needs. You get in line to check out. Then out of nowhere, before you've even placed the first box of cereal on the counter, the cashier looks up at you and says, "That will be $280." You say, "For what? I haven't checked out yet!". She replies, "For the person in front of you. They said that they wanted you to pay for their groceries."

Feel violated? How about taken advantage of? How about yes, to both of those! Why? The location is right. You are at the checkout. The action is right. This is the place you pay for what is in your cart. What is missing? Relationship. If the person in front of you were your father, mother, brother, sister, pastor, child or friend and they needed help with their grocery bill and you could help, you most certainly would. However, insert an unknown person in front of you and suddenly the narrative changes completely. Why? No relationship. You don't know them or their situations. You have no connection with their motive. Yet, in sales situations, we expect people we do not know and have not invested time to build an honest relationship with, to spend hundreds, thousands or even millions of dollars without the security and safety of relationship.

Relationships existed before there was trade - in fact, it's what the bedrock of commerce was originally built upon. For example, let's imagine a man named James Greene. James is a cattleman. He knows a man, Thomas Southard, who is a shepherd. Thomas knows Robert Trenton, who is a carpenter. James needs a carpenter to build a new barn. Thomas has just ewed 3 lambs and needs a shelter. Robert has decided to begin raising a few sheep for the wool and milking a cow for his family. Robert agrees to build a new barn in exchange for a milk cow and the shelter for the 3 lambs. All parties' needs are met through relationships. Sales begin in relationships and are fueled by the meeting of needs. Nothing more, nothing less. I can hear someone thinking, *I am not a cattleman, shepherd or carpenter and I don't need any of those things, so how does this apply to me?* Let's look at this a little more closely and examine the application for modern day.

The buyer has needs. The seller has needs. Since this book is for the sales professional, let's look at this from your perspective. Your need is your income. You need to make an income to sustain yourself and possibly your family. You have exclusive rights to a particular product or service. The only way a customer is going to get access to these products and services is through you. Conversely, the buyer has needs. They have identified you as the purveyor of a particular product or service that may be able to help them achieve their objectives. An introduction and a genuine desire to meet their needs are the two foundational ingredients to a mutually beneficial relationship. We talk far too much about closes, deals, special sales, yes/no questions and gimmicks. This is why the profession of sales has taken such a hit to its reputation. Remember the snake oil salesman? When competition threatened his edge, he had to change his tactics from quality of products to quantity of claims. The more outlandish the claims, the better chance he had to close the sale. Then came the closing techniques, destroying the very fabric of why sales existed to begin with. A total stranger doesn't call me and ask me to help him install a new bathroom cabinet. My father does. And I will help him gladly. Why? Relationship. If the total stranger would like for me to help him install his bathroom cabinet, then we will begin by building a relationship. Salespeople today are trained to skip the most important starting place for all true, successful, profitable sales. It seems like these days we're met with statements like, "What brings you to the car lot today? On a day this beautiful, I know you didn't just come to look." Or something like, "Well, you know you really came to the appliance store with the intention of leaving here with something, right?" *Stop closing!* Geez. How about you take a few minutes to really get to know me and what I need? How about you really ask because it matters to you? How about you invest in me even if I don't buy from you? When we see your genuine concern and desire to help us with our needs, we will buy. Maybe not today, but we will buy. We know you have sales goals. We know you need commissions to survive. That matters to us, too - but not at the expense of, or in place of a real relationship. *I don't mean get all up in people's lives or engage with them in an overly-invasive way.* I don't mean crash Thanksgiving dinner. I mean initiate a genuinely compassionate, professional relationship. So here is a challenge for you, the reader. The next time you clock in or go to your sales job, forget everything else you think you know about successful engagement with prospects. Forget how behind you are on the sales board. Forget how far ahead the next salesperson is for the month or week or even day. I challenge you to focus on one simple thing: every chance you have to encounter another human being, I want you to see them as just that. A human being. Not a sale. Not a bonus. Not a closing challenge. Not another lay down or slam. See them as your neighbor who has a genuine need. They may not be ready for the need to be met. That's ok. You wouldn't pressure your grandmother into something - so why do it to a stranger? You would wait for your grandmother to be fully ready. If the prospect isn't ready, your only mission today is to make sure they have all the right *and* accurate information to make the best decision for their family. Educate them. Give them reading material; homework, even. No pressure. Just education - because you're the expert right? Prove it. Build a relationship based on a genuine desire to meet their needs. Lay the cornerstone of all true and long term sales: relationship. Then follow up with them to see if the information helped. If not, then get them more information. If you will do this, and prove that your concern is genuine and not superficial and shallow, when the time comes for a purchase, they *will* come back to you because you have earned their trust. Period. Not only that, but they will tell everyone they know that they have finally found someone who genuinely cares. Yeah, it will be more work than you are used to, but people are worth it. You are worth it. Start at the beginning. Where it all started. Relationship.

NOTES & TAKEAWAYS

1. In your experience, describe a time when relationship was the driving force in your desire to help someone in need.

2. In your experience, describe a time when genuine relationship was absent in a sales engagement.

3. Can you remember an experience where a relationship was built *before* a sales engagement took place? If so, please describe here:

CHAPTER 7

E = Empathy

Empathy. I remember the first time I heard someone explain the difference between sympathy and empathy. It made me realize the power of empathy vs. sympathy and I wanted to be the one who could share empathy. Sympathy, while important, seemed so detached. Whatever was said from the perspective of sympathy was too sterile, too segregated, too insulated from the actual being able to help. In my opinion, sympathy is the city slicker who watched the farmer hand plowing a field, drenched in sweat, exhausted and thirsty, and says, "That poor farmer. Look how hard he is working. I sure do feel bad for him. But when the harvest comes, I will be first in line to pick up my bushel basket overflowing with the fruits of his labor." While sympathy has its place, empathy is infinitely more powerful. Empathy sees the farmer drenched with sweat, thirsty, tired, and says, "I'm going to take that farmer a tall glass of cold water and let him rest a minute because I have plowed my own fields and I know exactly how exhausted he feels right now." Empathy *identifies* with the person or person's situation because they are intimately acquainted with pain, struggle, need, or joy from a personal experience of their own. Empathy is impossible if you haven't "been there". This is as critical as any of the other letters in this lesson. You must be able to identify, personally, with the need in order to meet the need efficiently and effectively. Earlier in the book, I mentioned the root of need and the fruit of impact. Empathy means that you are able, in a relevant meaningful way, to identify with the root of your customer's need, and the fruit of how the need impacts their lives. To use the example of my mother and her inhalers again, I am intimately acquainted with the root of the need she has for her medication. The impact of the need not being met is that I may lose my mother to an inability to breathe if she doesn't get her medication. I am intimately acquainted with both the root of need and the fruit of impact. Now, let's look at the car example. This fits every buying situation, by the way. I will show you what I mean.

A middle aged lady parks in the guest parking lot of the local dealership. She exits the car and you happen to be the one to see her arrive. You make your way to her location and the introduction begins. What you discover is that she is a single mother, her old car has finally died and the one she is driving is borrowed from a neighbor. The car she is borrowing has to be returned at the end of the day and she hopes she can find a car by then to get her 2 small children to daycare and herself to work. **Root:** she needs a car for imperative transportation. She has two small children so it needs to accommodate the passengers, probably both in car seats. **Fruit:** if she doesn't get a car soon, she will most likely lose the children's spot as daycare as well as eventually lose her job and only source of income. You know the rest of the story. While you may have never been in her position, you can offer her empathy because you have researched enough with her that you can identify with the root of her need and the fruit of the impact in her life if her need isn't met. Changes the game, right? Now you aren't thinking about commissions and being salesperson of the month. You are a salesperson on a mission to meet the need and diffuse the impact.

Now, some of you may be saying, "What if the prospect is wealthy and there isn't a need?" Glad you asked. There is still the root of need and the fruit of impact. The root of his need may be that he or she has driven a Toyota Prius their entire career. They have recently received a promotion for all of their hard work and that came with a hefty bonus. Their spouse or partner has given them the greenlight to reward their labor with a new sports car. Something with a little growl and muscle. Where is the root and fruit in this scenario? *Root* of need is the right to validate many long hours behind the desk or machine or heavy machinery, and the *fruit* of impact is that if they don't find a way to reward themselves for the many years of faithful commitment to their work, they could easily find themselves on the precipice of occupational disaster from lack of validation. Risk/Reward is a real thing. When a person asserts risk day in and day out and doesn't see a reward, they begin to lose morale and motivation. We see it in the workplace everywhere. While your car lot may not have the right growl and muscle, you can certainly identify with the root of need and the fruit of impact. What if you came to work day in and day out and never received an "attaboy" or "attagirl" from your superiors? What if on every pay day when checks were being handed out, your name was never called? What if your direct deposit never showed in your account? Risk/Reward. You risk your value in the marketplace to earn a living. No risk, no reward. See? They are really not looking to throw their money around. They are simply looking for the reward they have earned for all the years of risk. Investing themselves in a career or a company or a cause. The reward to them will come in a package with 420-HP under the hood.

Conversational sales must be powered by empathy. What is empathy? An intimate understanding of the root of need and the fruit of impact if the need is satisfied. Take the time to identify with the need and impact of your customers through the art of listening. Stop talking so much and listen. Seriously. They will unpack the root and fruit for you if you will just listen. Then, you can proceed to the next step in powerful conversational sales: *action*.

NOTES & TAKEAWAYS

1. Define Empathy:

2. Why is empathy important in a sales engagement?

3. In your experience, describe a time when empathy was the driving force in one of your sales engagements.

CHAPTER 8

A = Action

Action. It's in short supply it seems. It is the one thing about me that I think rattles some of the people who work with me. One thing that I just can't stand is an imbalance between talk and action. In other words, I am not the guy who likes to sit through meetings that talk about action - I am the guy who likes to put action into motion. I have always been that way and sometimes it has proven to be my achilles heel. What I mean by that is sometimes, I don't talk enough about the action, only to find out too late that something could have been talked through or troubleshooted more. But remember, businesses are not exactly overrun with people who are action-oriented; they are more overrun with people who love to talk about ideas but few want to take the initiative to bust their knuckles getting it done. So, at the end of the day, I guess I'm more of a "get it done" kind of person than a "let's talk about getting it done" kind of person … and I am okay with that. I get along well with that part of myself.

Now, let's talk about action as it relates to conversational sales. We have already established the relationship. We also understand the importance of empathy. So, now what?

Action.

The doing of what needs to be done. Not delegating; but rather, putting your own sweat on the towel and getting it done. Oh yes, this is the part that really gets me motivated. The "stop running your trap and roll up your sleeves and get busy" part. Can you see I'm an action guy? Am I enjoying this too much? I can say it a few other ways if you need me to.

Oh, you get it? Okay then, I digress.

When you have clearly established the relationship (and there must be one), and you have intimately identified with the need, then the next step is the meeting of that need. You are the bridge between the need and the need, met. If all you see when you have reached this place in the sales cycle is a commission or a bonus or a plaque for the month, then you might as well pack up your things, buy a shovel and do something honorable until you can see past your own ambitions to the needs of those around you. It's not about you. It's about them. And when you learn to love your neighbor as yourself, which apparently is a heckuva lot, then you will finally begin to see that meeting the needs of others is the only truly satisfying path to your goals and ambitions. *period.*

The need has been made clear. You must rise to the occasion and provide the precise solution to the problem. Not too much. Not too little. If you have done your homework, as we have previously discussed, then you know why the need exists, what will resolve the need, and how to ensure the need remains met for the foreseeable future. You know what the budget *really* is. You have the full picture. You are now a surgeon. A master of irrefutable value. At this moment, you can literally impact a life indefinitely. I would say in modern-day sales, some sort of action isn't scarce. Sales are happening somewhere, every minute of every day. The action that I am calling sales professionals to strive for is precise action. I refer to it as "surgical action". What do I mean by this phrasing? I mean beyond the commitment to action is the equally important promise that when the customer goes home with your product or service, they will not wake up in several days wondering why or how they ended up with your product or service. They will not experience any remorse because of the time you took to accurately define their needs and prescribed resolution for those needs. You will have done this together. You clearly discussed all associated costs. You drilled down to ground zero and made sure they were receiving *exactly* what they needed. This is surgical action. The problem with the sales landscape today is that successful sales, or the "action" part of keeping it **R.E.A.L.**, is quantified and valued in the amount of "upsell" and "add-ons" that one can accomplish. If you are reading this book, whether victim or perpetrator, you know what this is and how it feels. There are sales organizations that actually promote and reward upselling and add-ons, even when they aren't necessary. Look, I believe that informing a customer or client that what they are looking at buying may underserve or fall short of meeting the clearly expressed needs. I believe it is our duty to educate and inform our customers and clients as to all the options available to them. But overselling is a huge cardinal sin in this system that I am teaching you. Overselling is a sure fire way to provoke buyer's remorse and cultivate distrust.

I used my mother in a previous example and now I will use my grandfather. The relationship I have with my grandfather lays the perfect groundwork for explaining empathy. Empathy lays the foundation for action. Action builds the framework of trust, one brick (action) at a time. When he tells me his need, for example, is that his blood pressure is up, I don't go to the corner drugstore and bring back 17 possible remedies for his blood pressure. I bring back *exactly* what will work to restore his health as quickly as possible. Now, an appropriate "add-on" would be my recommendation that he take a garlic pill with his breakfast each day and a brisk walk around his entire yard every afternoon - these would both be excellent compliments to his medication. How do I know? From personal experience. I have an enlarged heart. This can sometimes cause my blood pressure to spike. When this happens, I take garlic pills, drink lots of water, and walk around the farm as a daily routine until my blood pressure normalizes. It usually takes 2 -3 days. See, I am in a unique position to offer an add-on to the exact solution for his current need. How? Experience. Get it? If you don't have experience with the add-on you are offering, then all you have to base your offering on is glorified gossip. Hearsay. Book knowledge. Not experiential evidence. I hope this is hitting home. Do you have experiential evidence that the add-on will actually improve the customer or client's experience? Enrich their lives further? If not, all you can do is pass on the hearsay and hearsay you pass on, will come back to you. Remember that. Be a surgeon of sales. When you take action, take it specifically. Precisely. Offer the available add-ons that you believe in or understand from experience. Provide all the information that's available so that an educated and logical decision can be made. But, never, never pressure an upsell. Would you upsell to your ill grandfather? I wouldn't. If you would, maybe you should look deeper than this book to see why your sales career rings closer to organized crime and highway robbery instead of the humble, honorable, integrity-built, needs-driven occupation it was intended to be.

NOTES & TAKEAWAYS

1. Define action as we talked about it in this chapter.

2. Can action be accurate without relationship and empathy?

3. In your experience, please describe a time in your life when action was fueled by both relationship AND empathy.

CHAPTER 9

L = Life

What an interesting term to use when describing relationships. Do you consider your long-term relationships as giving life? I'm sure you are thinking of some relationships that squash life. Ones that strangle the life out of every moment encountered. I also hope you are thinking of at least a few relationships that bring life. The ones that are elixir when you are wounded, cold water when you are thirsty, a warm embrace when you're lonely. The ones you can't imagine life without. There it is. The ones you can't imagine life without. This is the final stop on our journey to understanding the origin and destination of genuine conversational sales.

Go back in your mind for a minute. Think back to salespeople in your past who fit this description. A person of character and poise in the face of your uncertainty. A truly reliable rock. Or maybe you can't remember one. Are you one? We all remember the romantic scenes of our favorite movies where one looks at another in a tender moment and says, "I can't imagine my life without you." I am not suggesting that salespeople should go into work every day expecting to hear this from their customers and clients. I am suggesting that the sentiment can and should most certainly be present, in its own way. Here is what I mean:

Too often in my career I have heard salespeople refer to a "deal" or a "close" that was maybe oversold or upsold far too much. While they were high-fiving the other salespeople for the highest grossing sale of the day, they were saying under their breath, "I hope they don't hate me in the morning." I have heard so many stories from supposed "successful salespeople" as to their utter dread that they may see the customer at the grocery store, or at church, or at the ballgame for fear that they might be called out on their gross overshot of sale-vs-need. I recall a conversation with a new car dealership GM who point blank told me that he knew his sales team was actively overselling cars to customers, knowing that within 90-days, the cars would be repossessed due to the customer's inability to afford it. *And he didn't care.* He explained that the manufacturer had quotas he had to meet and if he needed to pick up a few cars, it was a small price to pay in order to hit his sales goals. There was no acknowledgement of the toll this would take on the unsuspecting buyer. No remorse for the devastation the buyer would experience when they stepped outside one cold morning to head to work only to find their car missing. I know, this isn't you - at least, I hope it's not you; however, it's someone out there - right now- filling out the paperwork on a deal that will wreak havoc on the lives of the ones who fall for it.

This is not life. This is not integrity. Back in the era when sales was finding its legs, this would have brought a thorough beating and several nights in the town square's stock-and-chains. Because we are no longer there, but here in 2021, how do we make the transition from where we are now into a framework of integrity-driven sales that provoke thoughts of confidence and trust? A place where people can depend on the sales profession to provide them with exactly what they need and not a shred more? A place where salespeople invest enough time in a prospect to deeply understand their genuine needs and endeavor to meet that need with surgical precision?

Life in the context of this book simply means that when the sale is over, the sales person remains a steady rock and anchor of dependability when it comes to their product or service. Someone the customer can look to, *for life*. It may not be every month. It may not be every year. But when the time comes, the customer can count on the salesperson for genuine truth and precise assistance with their needs. Life also means that I, as the salesperson, will make sure that your needs remain my priority for the rest of my career and beyond. I want you to know that as long as I am able to help you, I will. I am going to be here. When you need your next car, I will be here. When you need your next appliance, I will be here. When you need to buy your next home, I will be here. You can count on me to be honest and truthful with you. This is life.

In the example of my grandfather and his blood pressure medicine, I won't just drop it off, grab a cold soda out of his fridge and roll out wishing him luck. Because of our relationship, I empathize with his condition. Because of my empathy, I take prompt and precise action. And after the action has been taken, I make sure he is taking his medicine properly. I also check up on him regularly. Why? Because he matters to me. In my business, my clients matter to me. I don't just cash the check and wish them luck. My commitment is to stay with them every step of the way. We are in this together. If I miss something, I will acknowledge it and do my best to make it right. If I oversell, I will make it right. If I undersell, I will make it right. To the very best of my ability, I will. I am not going anywhere. We will experience this new product or service together. And where this journey of product or service begins and ends, we will do this together. This is life. Will you be brave enough to do life with your customers and clients instead of hit and run? I challenge you to do just that. Every step - every mile.

NOTES & TAKEAWAYS

1. Define life in relation to a sales engagement.

2. Is life possible without relationship, empathy, and action?

3. In your experience, describe a time when you or a salesperson exercised this type of ongoing care, after the sale.

CHAPTER 10

The Greatest Gift

Almost home. The setting sun has blanketed the mountain sky with a red and orange hue that looks as if it were ablaze with wildfire. The farm animals are getting quiet and the crickets and bullfrogs are tuning their instruments for a nighttime sonata. The day's work has ended and just over the ridge, I can see the lights of home. A beacon of safety, love and family. It calls to me. I can hear the rocks and white mountain dirt under my feet. A briskness is in the air. In the near distance I can hear the creek, singing its never ending song. The tree tops sway in the breeze, much like a child, happy to see a parent coming home. Hands are blistered and back is sore, but the day was not wasted. Though strength was tested and toughness challenged, another day has proven productive. I can see a shadow moving in the lighted house. Through the curtains I see the movements of one who has prepared a meal fit for kings and tonight I will feast as a king. I can smell the fragrance of homemade bread dancing on the wind toward me as a siren of the sea. The song is sweet and beckoning. My pace picks up just a bit as I can almost taste the apple butter from last fall's harvest. Turning the corner at the fence line and heading down the footpath to the back door, I can hear my mamaw say, "Grant, reckon Gale will be here soon? Supper is ready and I don't want that youngun to eat a cold supper." Pappaw responds, "I'm sure he will turn up directly, Faye." A smile breaks across my lips, even now, as I remember these treasured moments.

The one thing I haven't covered is the starting point of all great character. Your genesis. Your beginning. Your story. I have just walked with you over the ridge and up the dirt road where my story began. We all have different stories, and they all matter. You may not have many fond memories of your childhood. You might have nothing but pain in your past or not even remember much about your past. You might feel like your past is something you would like to forget, altogether. Maybe you *have* forgotten it. But I want you to consider the greatest gift your past has to offer. Without this gift, your future would be empty. Your present would be meaningless. It is a gift that no one else can claim. It has been assigned to only one and only one can grow from it. The gift your past has given this world is: *you.*

If you are reading this book, your past has gifted the world with the you that is right here, right now. It has shaped you and formed you. It has led you to this moment, holding this book, considering the thoughts in its pages. And no matter what you think about your past, it has given you the opportunity to be who you are and it has been the teacher for what you have learned.

If your past is difficult to look at, remember it didn't keep you. It's in the past. You are not what you did or what was done to you. You are here now. The next moment is up to you. Will you stumble forward with your eyes fixed behind you, or will you give it all a proper burial and step out into a new day with new life and new hope?

If your past is beautiful, will you glean character-building bricks and mortar from every moment and erect a monument to honor the people who brought you here? This chapter is titled, *The Greatest Gift*, and it is so titled for a reason. I named it that because I want each reader to realize that the greatest gift in all conversational sales is the person who looks back at them from the mirror. You, the one reading this right now, you are the greatest gift. Religious or not, the Bible is full of practical wisdom and guidance for life, love and happiness. In the Old Testament, we see Abraham building an altar, or monument, every time God did something amazing for him and his family. This was to remind him (and the generations that would follow him), that God had done something amazing for him there, and when they found it on their travels, they would stop and resound Abraham's gratitude for the goodness of God in that place. Sometimes, they dug a well in the place where God had answered prayer. This well was to bless the travelers as they passed. While drinking from its cold waters, the travellers would thank God for the thing that He had done there and for inspiring Abraham to dig a well for their blessing, too. Maybe think of your past as a well, as well. Whether it is good or bad. It is a place where others can see the journey you have had and stop to appreciate the man or woman you have become. The decision before you is this: to either remain on the sales road you were travelling when you picked this book up, or you can choose to self-evaluate, making sure that you are on the very best and highest road possible. Hopefully, your self-reflection will reveal that you are already walking out the suggestions put forth in this book; however, a number of you may realize that your path needs to lead back to the best and highest pathway and you can see the importance and urgency to do so. Wherever you might be at this point, I just want to make sure you understand that while your past doesn't define you, it does serve the purpose of getting you from there to here, so make sure you take the time to evaluate your whole journey, glean the very best lessons it offers, purpose to move on from here in authenticity - then dig a well to give thanks and get back on your way with the very best you, in tow! The ones who come after you will drink from your well for years to come and give thanks, too!

I have been known to say that I can teach anyone who can talk, to sell. If you are able to have a conversation regarding something you are passionate about, you can sell. I still believe that. I am convinced that true, genuine sales have nothing to do with closes and scripts. They have everything to do with *you*; everything to do with your desire to meet the genuine need of another human being. No matter how many seminars you have been to or how many audio books you have listened to or read - will you decide, today, to return to the original architect's design for your profession? Will you commit yourself to looking past quotas and plaques to meet the customer where they are? If you will, this simple decision will transform your career in ways you never imagined. And, you will be able to go home at the end of the day knowing that your customers will be your customers for *life*. I challenge you and all members of the sales profession: endeavor right now and for the rest of your career to keep it ... **R.E.A.L.**.

R = Relationship

E = Empathy

A = Action

L = Life

NOTES & TAKEAWAYS

1. What is the greatest gift in any sales situation?

2. What does R.E.A.L. stand for?

3. What is the greatest lesson you have taken away from this book?

Epilogue

Lest anyone think that I believe myself to be the only person practicing **L.I.F.E.** and the only salesperson in possession of these truths, I want to assure you that I do not and am not. I know that there are many salespeople out there who are instinctively putting these truths into practice every day; even if they haven't written down like I have. It always does my heart so much good when I randomly encounter these sales professionals and it gives me hope that spreading **L.I.F.E.** is, indeed, possible. I thought it might be encouraging to share a recent example of such a sales professional with you, so you can see the whole cycle as it impacted me, the buyer, in this case.

I purchased a farm in 2020. It's not too many miles outside of a major city in North Carolina; however, it is just far enough out to have caused me a huge issue with regards to dependable internet and cable service. I did what anyone else would have done: I started making phone calls. I ended up reaching a gentleman with a company whose name is known to everyone reading this epilogue and this gentleman, (we'll call him, Justin) kindly listened as I began telling him why I was calling. When I paused to let him respond, Justin said, "I hear what you are saying and I'm so sorry that you've had so much trouble finding a solution. I tell you what, we're trying out a new program that feels a little old school, but how would you feel about me coming out to your place and sitting down with you to find out a little more about everything you are needing?" Well, you've read my book now, so you can only imagine how I responded. I said, "Are you kidding me? That would be fantastic! Thank you!" I cannot express how much my anxiety began to subside - and Justin hadn't even gotten to the farm yet! It made me feel like he had really listened to my needs and he wanted to invest in the relationship piece - enough so, that he was going to come all the way to my residence. The next day, Justin arrived and sat with me, asking all the pertinent questions and making furious notes while I gave him my answers. After he had a good understanding of everything I needed, he sprang into action. He immediately identified things that he felt would serve my family best, as well as informed us of some things we needed that he wasn't sure he could accommodate. He walked around outside to identify areas of entry for possible service and he made a couple of calls to discuss our unique challenges with his manager. He left the house about 2 hours later with a comprehensive list of everything we truly needed and set time to call us the next afternoon. The next morning, way ahead of the scheduled call back time, my phone rang and much to my surprise, it was Justin. He said, "I was up half the night thinking about your situation. I know that we're going the route we talked about yesterday; but after thinking about it, I'm just not sure that is going to meet your needs the way I want it to. I know this is outside the box, but I think you'd be better off if we went with ____ from us and let's maybe contact _____ about helping you with the other." Well, my friends, "_____ with the other" was not with the company he represented. Justin genuinely cared about meeting my family's needs to the point that he sacrificed some of the business he would get because he realized that his products would likely not bring complete satisfaction. Honestly, I was speechless. When it was all said and done, Justin made 2 more visits to our home, connected us with the other company to fulfill the piece he thought they'd handle better and then signed us up with the company he represented for the rest. I can tell you, without a doubt, we could have had no greater guide for our internet and streaming journey than Justin. He shared **L.I.F.E.** with us and it was absolutely, life-giving. So, that is what I'm talking about in this book. I have been the seller and I have been the buyer. These are the types of engagements that lead to longevity and great memories. Add to this narrative, my friends. Become a part of *this* story. It will change you, for good.